W9-AMN-557

Chimpanzees

Learning Resources Center
Jordan High School
Jordan, Minnesota

Chimpanzees

social climbers of the forest

Tamsin Constable

42677

London, New York, Sydney, Dehli, Paris, Munich, and Johannesburg

Publisher: Sean Moore
Editorial director: LaVonne Carlson
Project editor: Barbara Minton
Editor: Jennifer Quasha
Art editor: Gus Yoo
Production director: David Proffit

First published in 2000 by
BBC Worldwide Ltd,
Woodlands, 80 Wood Lane, London W12 0TT

Text, design and illustrations
© BBC Worldwide Ltd 2000

All rights reserved. No part of this book may be reproduced in
any form or by any means, without permission in writing from
the publisher, except by a reviewer who may quote brief passage
in a review.

ISBN 0-7894-7153-1

Produced for BBC Worldwide by Toucan Books Ltd, London

Printed and bound in France by Imprimerie Pollina s.a. - n°81933-C

Color separations by Imprimerie Pollina s.a.

PICTURE CREDITS:
Page 3 BBC Natural History Unit Picture Library/Karl Amman.
6 Photo Researchers Inc/ Tom McHugh. 9 Olive Pearson. 10 Ardea/Ferrero-Labat.
11 Minden/Gerry Ellis, T; Ardea/Adrian Warren, B.
12 Wayne Ford/Wildlife Art Limited.
13 BBC Natural History Unit Picture Library/Karl Amman. 14 Minden Pictures/ Frans Lanting. 15 Ardea/Adrian Warren. 17 Ardea/Adrian Warren. 18 Magnum Photos/ Michael K. Nichols. 18-19 BBC Natural History Unit Picture Library/Karl Amman. 19 Photo Researchers Inc/Kenneth W. Fink, BR. 20 Minden Pictures/ Gerry Ellis. 21 Oxford Scientific Films/Jackie Le Fevre. 22 A.B.P.L./ M. Harvey/Gallo Images. 22-23 NHPA/Gerard Lacz. 24 The Jane Goodall Institute-UK/ adapted from *The Chimpanzees of Gombe: Patterns of Behaviour* by Jane Goodall. 25 BBC Natural History Unit Picture Library/Karl Amman,T; Gallo Images/ M. Harvey, B. 26 Ardea/Ferrero-Labat. 27 NHPA/Steve Robinson. 28 Ian Redmond. 29 NHPA/Nigel J. Dennis. 30 A.B.P.L./ Anup Shah/Gallo Images. 33 A.B.P.L./ M. Harvey. 34-35 NHPA/ M. Harvey. 36 Oxford Scientific Films/Clive Bromhall. 37 A.B.P.L./Nigel J. Dennis. 38 Wayne Ford/Wildlife Art Limted/The Jane Goodall Institute-UK/adapted from *The Chimpanzees of Gombe: Patterns of Behaviour* by Jane Goodall. 39 BBC Natural History Unit Picture Library/Karl Amman. 40 BBC Natural History Unit Picture Library/Karl Amman. 41 BBC Natural History Unit Picture Library/ Anup Shah. 42 Photo Researchers Inc/Tom McHugh, T, B. 43 NHPA/Alan Williams. 44 Gallo Images/M.Harvey. 45 Ardea/Adrian Warren, T, B. 46 BBC Natural History Unit Picture Library/Karl Amman. 47 Gallo Images/M. Harvey. 48-49 DRK Photo/M.Harvey. 50 BBC Natural History Unit Picture Library/Karl Amman.
51 The Jane Goodall Institute-UK/adapted from *Chimpanzees of Gombe: Patterns of Behaviour* by Jane Goodall. 52 Minden Pictures/Frans Lanting. 55 Minden Pictures/Gerry Ellis. 56 NHPA/ Christopher Ratier. 57 Courtsey of Frans de Waal from *Chimpanzee Politics*. 58 The Jane Goodall Institute-UK/C. Packer. 59 NHPA/Steve Robinson. 60 The Jane Goodall Institute-UK/adapted from *The Chimpanzees of Gombe: Patterns of Behaviour* by Jane Goodall. 61 Oxford Scientific Films/Clive Bromhall, T; DRK Photo/Kennan Ward, B. 62-63 Oxford Scientific Films/ Survival Anglia/Jackie Le Fevre. 64-65 The Jane Goodall Institute-UK/P. McGinnis. 66 Oxford Scientific Films/Martyn Colbeck. 67 Minden Pictures/Frans Lanting. 68 Oxford Scientific Films/Animal Animals/ Dani Jeske. 71 Oxford Scientific Films/Michael W. Richards. 72 NHPA/Steve Robinson. 73 Oxford Scientific Films/Clive Bromhall. 74 Oxford Scientific Films/Stan Osolinski. 75 Ardea/ Adrian Warren. 76 Minden Pictures/Gerry Ellis. 77 Magnum Photos/Michael K. Nichols. 78 Oxford Scientific Films/Clive Bromhall. 79 Magnum Photos/ Michael K. Nichols. 80 BBC Natural History Unit Picture Library/Karl Amman. 81 Ian Redmond, TL; BBC Natural History Unit Picture Library/ Anup Shah, BR.
82 Ardea/Adrian Warren.
83 Wayne Ford/Wildlife Art Limited.
84 Ardea/Adrian Warren. 85 DRK Photo/Kennan Ward. 86-87 Ian Redmond.
88 Ardea/Ferrero-Labat.
89 Minden Pictures/Frans Lanting. 90 The Jane Goodall Institute-UK/E.Tsolo/from *Through A Window* by Jane Goodall, Weidenfeld and Nicolson, 1990. 91 Minden Pictures/Gerry Ellis. 92 BBC Natural History Unit Picture Library/John Sparks. 93 Magnum Photos/Chris Steele Perkins.

Contents

FOREST CREATURES

FOREST CREATURES

A sunbeam pierces the forest canopy and glances down the long, mossy trunk of a tall tree. Broken up by tiers of leaves, the mosaic of soft light settles on the tiny face of a three-month-old chimpanzee curled up against its mother in a night nest. In a nearby nest, a four-year-old female awakes and edges down the tree trunk to the ground, where she plays with another youngster. The mother sits up and stretches, careful not to squash her infant. Then she suddenly stands up. The baby clenches its fists tightly, gripping onto a handful of her mother's belly fur, and clamps herself closely for the swift climb down.

At the bottom of the tree, the mother grooms her infant while she waits for her exuberant older daughter. She is good at waiting. This is her third infant, and she has had plenty of opportunity to learn how to mother. Her eldest, a male aged 13, is now fully independent and making his own way in the community.

Previous page: Chimpanzees and humans share a now-extinct common ancestor, the so-called missing link. The fossil record shows that it was more chimpanzee-like than human. In comparison with humans, who have evolved a lot in the past 5 million years or so, chimpanzees have changed relatively slowly.

A DAY IN THE LIFE ...

A family of chimpanzees wanders through the forest, climbing trees to find food. They spend several hours up in the trees. In between, the adult female sometimes rests on the ground. In the late morning, the female suddenly stops still, listening carefully. There it is again. A volley of pant-hoot calls from a crowd of chimpanzees a quarter of a mile away. By the sound of it, they have found a huge fruit tree. She steps up the pace and her daughter has to hurry to keep up.

When they arrive at the huge fig tree half an hour later, about 20 chimpanzees are gorging themselves on the soft figs, grunting their enjoyment. The female's eldest son is up in the branches with his "gang," the two other males with whom he spends increasing amounts of time. They are keeping a respectful distance away from the alpha male, who is keeping a close eye on a young female who is fertile at the moment. The female climbs up and greets the alpha male with a sharp, breathy "hah" as she crouches low and touches her open mouth to his arm. Then she moves away and starts to feed. Her daughter cannot quite reach some of the fruit, and so the mother hands her some of her own.

Another high-ranking male arrives. He greets the alpha male with elaborate respect, screaming with a fear grin and cowering low until the alpha reaches out and draws him near. The two males do not feed until they have groomed each other reassuringly for 10 minutes or so.

Suddenly, a deafening outburst shatters the peace. An adult male in peak condition crashes in. He has been challenging the alpha male for weeks now. Black hair bristling and shoulders hunched, he charges through the bushes, sending lower-ranking chimpanzees running from his path.

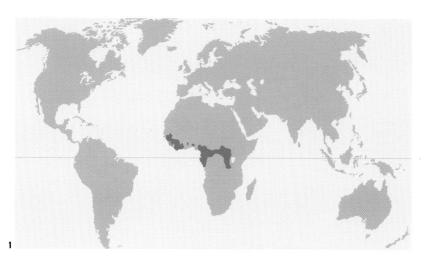

1. Chimpanzees are found in the forests and woodlands of western, central, and East Africa.

Learning Resources Center
Jordan High School
Jordan, Minnesota

The alpha male abandons his grooming and swings down out of the tree to a chorus of screams, barks, and hoots from the other members of his group. He directs a display of his own back at the insubordinate male hurls branches and rocks, and pounds on tree buttresses to reassert his authority. Only when the alpha male has settled the respect issue to his satisfaction do things calm down again. Chimpanzees make peace with each other, and the din subsides.

After eating their fill, several chimpanzees rest in the heat of the day. Little knots of animals in twos, threes, and fours groom. In mid afternoon, small groups start disappearing back into the forest. A female and her daughter move on up the hillside. The adolescent son joins them for the afternoon. They reach a small, fast-running stream, and the older male takes his sister on his back, jockey style, and jumps over it. On the other side, the female remembers that here is a huge termite mound. They cannot see it yet, but they are getting close. The female picks a long, slender stem that will make a perfect tool. When they reach the termite mound, the daughter watches as her mother strips the leaves

1

2

1. Thanks to the pincer movement made possible by their opposable thumbs, chimpanzees can pick and peel fruit such as these figs.

2. At Gombe, chimpanzees eat more termites than any other insect. It takes years of watching and trying before a young chimpanzee masters termite fishing.

 BEDTIME HANDICRAFT

Every night, a chimpanzee makes itself a fresh nest to sleep in. Young chimpanzees learn this craft from watching their mother. First, the chimpanzee chooses a tree, but not a food tree, with a stable branch for a base 9–12 yd from the ground. Then, the chimpanzee squats or stands up on this branch and pulls three more thick branches toward itself. It presses these under its feet and weaves them into a rough disc. The next step is to weave thinner branches into a wreath. The nest is now a strong, springy platform. All that is left is to make it comfortable by lining it with leaves and twigs. A skilled chimpanzee can build a nest in one minute.

from the flexible stem. The mother then scratches at the surface of the mound, and uncovers one of the hundreds of holes that leads into the labyrinth below. She pokes the stem in and wriggles it gently. The daughter chimpanzee picks up a short twig, bashes it ineffectively at the mud, and then wanders off to play with her big brother. Her mother, deep in concentration, slides her stem out again, taking enormous care not to knock off the dozen termites clinging to it. She draws the stem through her lips, scraping the insects into her mouth, and then bows low over the termite mound again for another dip.

After romping with his sister for a while, the male moves off a little way and waits. His mother ignores him. He stares at her, indicating that it is time they went. He is by no means a high-ranking male yet, but he is already dominant over all the females in the community, his mother included. So she gets up, scoops up her infant and follows him.

It is late, and the chimpanzees disappear back into the dusky forest. They find a suitable nesting tree and climb up. Within minutes, three comfortable nests have been made. As the forest darkens, the female grooms her baby until he falls asleep.

PRIMATE CLASSIFICATION: CHIMPANZEES

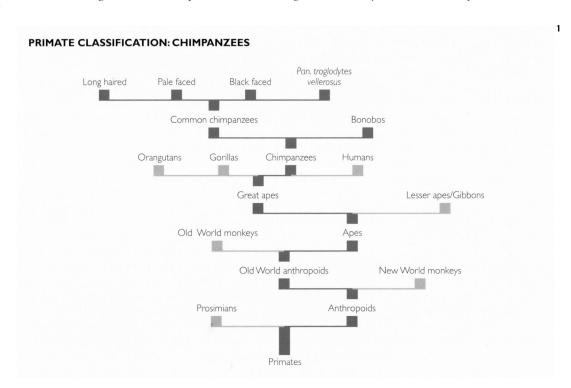

WHAT IS A CHIMPANZEE?

Chimpanzees fascinate humans. They are our closest living relatives and provide us with clues to our own evolutionary history. They are highly intelligent and can learn the rudiments of human vocabulary. Chimpanzees are interesting in themselves, however, not just as reflections of our own evolutionary past. Each chimpanzee is a unique, complex individual, adapted to solve the problems presented by both the ecological and social worlds in which it lives. Also, chimpanzees have something precious, a brain that is very big in relation to their body size. In particular, the part of the brain called the neocortex has enlarged over time. This is a thin layer of cells that lies over the two cerebral hemispheres and can be considered to be the "thinking" part of the brain. Thanks to their enlarged neocortex, chimpanzees are free from rigid patterns of behavior. They can be flexible in their responses to their environment. They can remember, try things out, make choices, and solve problems. They can even exploit their surroundings to a better effect.

Five great apes

The first apes evolved over 20 million years ago. There were many more ape species then than there are today, and many had lifestyles similar to those of modern-day monkeys. It was the evolution of the monkeys that was the downfall of most of the apes. Monkeys are able to eat both unripe and ripe fruits, where the apes are ripe-fruit specialists. Also,

2

1. Chimpanzees represent just two species among primates, which number more than 200 altogether.

2. A long childhood allows a chimpanzee's relatively big brain enough time to reach its full potential.

⭐ Over its lifetime, a chimpanzee will make 10,000 to 15,000 nests. Piled up, they would form a column 11 to 16 times the height of the Eiffel Tower in Paris.

because they were able to eat fruit at an earlier stage of their development, the monkey species were able to get more than their fair share of the available food. Eventually, they out competed the ape species.

Today there are only two families of apes: the lesser apes, or gibbons, and the five great apes: orangutans, gorillas, bonobos, chimpanzees, and humans. Humans, of course, live all over the world, while the rest of the great apes have a much more restricted distribution. Orangutans are found only in Southeast Asia, on the islands of Borneo and Sumatra. They are our distant relatives. Gorillas live in forests of West and central Africa, while our closest relatives, common chimpanzees and

bonobos, are found in the forests and woodlands of western, central, and East Africa.

When people think of a chimpanzee, the animal that they have in mind is probably a common chimpanzee, a misleading name since it is, in fact, rare. However, there is another species, the bonobo, sometimes called the pygmy chimpanzee, which is also an inappropriate name since it is not much smaller than the common chimpanzee. In the places where they live, bonobos are known as *bilia,* a name that some scientists prefer. In many ways the two species are alike. In fact, until 1929, they were thought to be the same species. Both have big ears, pouting lips, and brows that jut out above the eyes,

1

1. The rich supply of food in the dense rainforest means that bonobos can form large social groups of about 20, on average.

2. Traveling in small groups is the best way for common chimpanzees in Gombe to exploit the food supply.

and both live in big "fission-fusion" communities, groups that split into much smaller groups and then come together again. Look more closely, though, and the physical differences become clear.

The common chimpanzee

The common chimpanzee is stout, with a large head, broad shoulders, and a thick neck. Its arms are so long that, when it stands up, they reach below its knees. When the chimpanzee is on all fours, its head-to-body length is 30-36 in (77-92 cm) for males, 28-33 in (70-85 cm) for females. Its long arms make its back slope from the shoulders down to the hips. The male chimpanzee stands at 3-5.5 ft, (1-1.7 m) and the female is slightly smaller. Males weigh 75-154 lb (34-70 kg), and females weigh 57-110 lb (26-50 kg). They are extremely strong. An adult female could lift a 154 lb (70 kg) man with one

The other great apes are so similar to us that some scientists and philosophers call for certain basic human rights to be extended to all great apes.

hand. Their brain size is 300 to400 cc, in comparison with human brains which average 1400 cc.

Common chimpanzees are born with a pale face and jet-black hair. Over time, the skin on the face tends to darken to black, and the hair may lighten to dark brown. Hair grows in every direction, and both males and females may go bald in later life. Chimpanzees can live for 50 years.

Chimpanzees from various parts of Africa are different enough from one another that scientists split them into four subspecies, or populations that are geographically isolated and on their way to evolving into separate species. The four subspecies are the masked,or pale-faced, chimpanzee from West Africa, the black-faced chimpanzee from central Africa, the long-haired chimpanzee from East Africa, and *Pan troglodytes vellerosus,*which does

not yet have a common name, from Nigeria. Common chimpanzees can handle a wide range of habitats like thick rain forests, forests in hilly areas, savannas with patches of woodland, and even dry, flat savannas where evergreen trees are confined to a few gullies.

The bonobo

The bonobo is graceful and slender, with narrow shoulders and a thin neck. Its skull is small and round. Reddish lips and wide nostrils are set in a flat face, and the hair on the head is long and falls neatly on each side of a natural part. A bonobo also has long back legs, which lift its hips high and keep its body horizontal when it is on all fours. When a bonobo stands, it straightens up more

1. (opposite) The large gap between a chimpanzee's opposable big toe and the other toes is perfect for clinging to branches of all sizes.

 STRANDS OF EVIDENCE

Evolutionary scientists figure out how closely related two species are by looking at their DNA. Found in the nucleus of cells, DNA is the way in which genetic information is passed from parents to offspring. DNA is replicated as cells divide and an animal grows. Usually, the copy is flawless, but occasionally a tiny change, or a mutation, sneaks in. Over time, more and more mutations build up. Individuals of a species gradually drift further apart genetically. The difference in the DNA of any two species is evidence of how long ago they shared a common ancestor. Closely related species belong to the same genus. The difference between bonobos and common chimpanzees, both in the *Pan* genus, is 0.7 percent. Between gorillas, *Gorilla* genus, and common chimpanzees it is 2.3 percent. What about humans and chimpanzees? The difference is 1.6 percent, so the chimpanzee's closest relative is not the gorilla, It is us. It also means that humans should really be in the same genus as chimpanzees and bonobos.

than a common chimpanzee does. Bonobos are about the same head-to-body length as chimpanzees 28-33 in (70-83 cm), but less hefty. Males weigh 81-134 lb (37-61 kg) and females weigh 59-84 lb (27-38 kg). They have longer limbs and a smaller chest. Bonobos are restricted to the wet, equatorial virgin rain forest of the Democratic Republic of Congo and live in areas that are difficult to reach. There are not many left in the wild, 10,000 at the most, and probably even fewer.

Falling numbers

Ten thousand years ago, common chimpanzees were distributed all through the broad band of thick rain forest that traced the high-rainfall line of the Equator across Africa. The rainforest

covered some 2 million sq. mi (5 million sq. km), from the great lakes of Uganda, Tanzania, and Kenya to the Atlantic Ocean on the west coast. The rain forest is now being destroyed by logging and other forms of encroachment. The resulting fall in chimpanzee numbers has been dramatic and alarming. Only 60 years ago, there were probably several million chimpanzees spread almost all the way across Africa, from Gambia to Uganda, and south to Lake Tanganyika. Now, there are only some 200,000 (estimates vary from 150,000 to 235,000) left in the wild. Most live in the biggest undisturbed clumps of tropical rain forest across central Africa in the Democratic Republic of Congo, Cameroon, Congo Brazzaville, and Gabon. Chimpanzees have disappeared entirely from some countries.

 TIME IS RUNNING OUT

It may be only 10 to 20 years before chimpanzees are extinct in the wild. As well as habitat loss to agriculture, illegal logging in countries such as Gabon, in the Ivory Coast and central Congo destroys vast areas of forest every year. Chimpanzees are also threatened by the trade in wild animal meat. Though most chimpanzees used for research are now captive bred, baby chimpanzees are poached for the illegal pet trade and for other kinds of commercial exploitation. It is estimated that for every baby chimpanzee that arrives alive at its destination, another seven have died on the way.

1. Bonobos are more vocal than common chimpanzees and stretch their arms out when calling. Their voices are much shriller too.

2. Bonobos' faces are black at birth, but eventually lighten over time.

OREST LIFE

For chimpanzees, life in the forest is a series of challenges and choices: mating, bringing up young, defending territories, staying safe, developing, and maintaining social links. The list is almost endless. The top priority, though, is to find food. The entire area that a chimpanzee group occupies, known as a home range, must provide enough food for the whole community. For chimpanzees, food primarily means fruit. A rain forest, with plenty of fruit trees can provide for many chimpanzees within a small area, about 3 to 12 chimpanzees per sq mi (1 to 5 per sq km). Chimpanzees in this type of forest rarely need home ranges greater than 4 sq mi. (10 sq km.).

The more scattered the fruit trees, or the more seasonal the habitat, the bigger the home range needs to be. In thinner woodland, home ranges average 4-19 sq mi.(10-50 sq km), and in savanna areas, they average 46-58 sq mi.(120-150 sq km.) In Niokolo Koba National Park in Senegal, where there is only 3 percent forest cover, resources are so scarce

1. If a chimpanzee has not finished eating when the group moves on, it may break off a fruit-laden branch to take away.

2. By paying close attention to what others eat, young chimpanzees learn what is edible and what is not.

that even a home range of 129 sq mi. (333 sq km), the largest recorded, cannot support more than 25 to 30 chimpanzees. Chimpanzees in such places become nomadic, ranging over an area of 77-154 sq mi (200-400 sq km) and settling down temporarily whenever food is abundant.

Foraging groups

Communities of about 50 individuals have been seen in all three habitats, rain forest, woodland, and savanna, but anything from 15 to 80 chimpanzees live together in a single home range. However, they do not all travel together.

Even in areas where fruit trees are abundant, chimpanzees still face a problem finding food. Forest trees have distinctive fruiting seasons, which differ

Today, there are four subspecies of the common chimpanzee. However, in the early years of this century, there were as many as 14.

widely from species to species. Different trees of the same species may also fruit at different times, so it can be hard to predict whether fruit will be available. Trees also differ in how much fruit they bear and how good it is. This unpredictability in food availability and quality means that it does not make sense for huge bands of chimpanzees to travel together. If they find food, there is a chance that there will not be enough to go around, and if they do not find food, then the whole group loses out.

Common chimpanzee females usually forage alone or with young offspring. They have little to fear

1

2

1. Termite mounds present a mental and physical challenge to hungry chimpanzees.

2. Chimpanzees hate water and cannot swim, so trying to reach floating food is risky.

from predators, so they do not need to group together, and feeding alone reduces the competition for food. Sometimes, when food is abundant, a number of females, offspring, and males will form small, fluid feeding parties averaging 3 to 6 individuals. The size of these groups depends on the size of the fruit trees, the larger the trees, the larger the party. The presence of a fertile female can also influence party size by attracting males who wish to mate. These parties can last for anything from a few hours to a few days. The most dominant chimpanzee leads the way, so that in a small group even a low-ranking adolescent male may get a chance to practice being in charge. If a group finds a rich food source, the whole community of chimpanzees gathers together to share it.

Traveling around

All chimpanzees spend much of their time on the ground, following rough paths through the forest. They do not lean on the palms of their hands, as monkeys do, but instead make a half fist and let their knuckles take the weight. Knuckle walking may have

 MAPPING THE WAY

Chimpanzees build excellent mental maps of their home range. They remember where paths, streams, valleys, hills, look-out points, and good nesting trees are, and where they found good trees in the past. They can even infer, from finding ripe fruit in one place, where they might find the same kind of fruit elsewhere. They also have a clear idea of where they are and will often speed up a few minutes before they can see the food. Using these mental maps, chimpanzees can be flexible when they are deciding where to go. For example, they can choose a new route, going farther upstream to find a new crossing point if the water in a stream has risen.

evolved as a way of allowing great apes to keep the long fingers needed for clinging to branches while they gradually spent more time on the ground. Chimpanzees can walk upright on two legs, but not for very long. This is a useful way to take a few steps when they are carrying something. Some chimpanzees will tuck an object, such as a piece of fruit or wood, into their "pants pocket," the crease between their upper thigh and belly. The three legged hobble that follows is called crotch walking.

Then there is getting around above ground. Chimpanzees are good at swinging from branch to branch. This is useful if they are chasing a monkey or

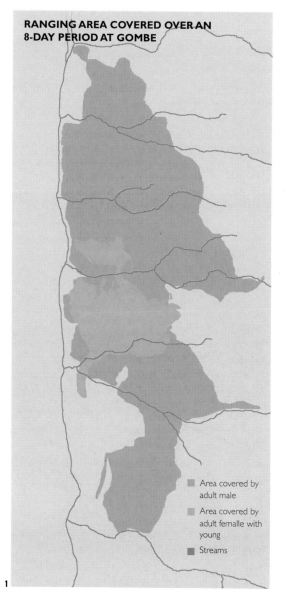

RANGING AREA COVERED OVER AN 8-DAY PERIOD AT GOMBE

Area covered by adult male

Area covered by adult femalle with young

Streams

1

1. Chimpanzees follow meandering paths while traveling within their home range. Here, the area covered by the female was less than that of the male, because she was accompanied by young.

2. Youngsters swing through the branches much more than adults, perhaps because their lighter bodies make brachiating much easier.

3. Knuckle walking and galloping are both efficient ways of traveling across rough terrain.

2

trying to avoid trouble below. Like all primates, chimpanzees are very much at home in the trees and can grip with their feet because their big toes are opposable (capable of being moved into a position facing the other toes), like thumbs.

How far chimpanzees travel in a day depends on many factors, such as how many are in the group, and whether there are any young or sick chimpanzees. Females tend to cover 1.25-2 mi (2-3 km) in a day, whereas males can manage nearly double that. But foraging distances can vary from as little as 1-9 mi (1.5-15 km). If males find a good source of fruit while out on one of the regular group excursions to

3

patrol the boundaries of their territory (to prevent chimpanzees from other communities encroaching), they sometimes lead females back there the following day. In the dense forests of Taï, chimpanzees regularly drum on the buttresses of trees with their hands and feet. The booming noise tells others where they are, where they are going, and how fast and how far they are traveling.

Bonanza!

When a subgroup of chimpanzees finds a tree (often a fig tree) laden with fruit, they often produce loud, excited pant-hoots. The more food there is, the more likely it is that chimpanzees will produce these calls, but it is not clear whether these pant-hoots are used to tell other chimpanzees that food is available, or if the chimpanzees are just very excited by their find.

Invitations or not, pant-hoots certainly bring other chimpanzees hurrying over to join the feed. With the double excitement of food and meeting up again with other chimpanzees, the party is raucous. Adult males, especially if they have not seen each other for a while, greet each other with wide-mouthed "grins" and noisy embraces. It can take some time before everyone settles down to gorge on the fruit.

These big food gatherings seem to trigger a shift in social relationships. Normally, only females share their food with their young, and then only if the food is out of the youngster's reach. But in a good fruit tree, it seems that the normal social hierarchy is temporarily suspended. Lower-ranking individuals pester others that they would never normally dare beg from. Begging involves holding an arm out stiff and straight, palm facing up, hand open, accompanied by persistent, staccato grunts. Because they

1. (opposite) Finding things to eat takes chimpanzees up to eight hours a day. Most foraging happens in the morning and early afternoon.

 DOCTOR APE

Chimpanzees sometimes seek out and eat a plant that they normally ignore. Instead of tugging off leaves at random, they select leaves, then roll them around in their mouths before swallowing them whole. The plant is called *Aspilia*, and as it passes through the gut, it scrapes out intestinal worms, which stick to the bristly leaves. *Aspilia* may also have antibiotic properties. Chimpanzees also occasionally eat dirt from termite mounds, often when they are known to have diarrhea. The soil is rich in two clay minerals, smectite and metahalloysite. Together, these minerals are similar to medicine used by humans to treat gut upsets.

1. A side salad of leaves helps the meat from a hunt go down.

2. Curious youngsters are forever poking around, fidgeting, and investigating.

⭐ When a chimpanzee walks upright, this is usually to free up a hand for carrying or throwing something.

do not store food and only rarely carry it, chimpanzees eat as much as possible whenever they have the opportunity. After the feast, stuffed, and sleepy, they usually rest for a while nearby. This gives them a chance to spend time socializing with individuals they might not have seen for some days, or even weeks.

Other food

Chimpanzees can eat as many as twenty different plant species in a single day, especially young leaves, and up to three hundred species in a year. Though fruit forms the bulk of their food (more than 60 percent over a year), it lacks protein and some essential minerals, so chimpanzees supplement it with leaves, blossoms, soft pith, galls, seeds, stems, bark, nuts, eggs, honey, and resin. This wild larder, which usually provides about 30 percent of a chimpanzee's diet, becomes increasingly important when there is less fruit available, when long dry seasons persist, for example. The last 10 percent of the chimpanzee diet consists of animal protein, mainly insects (in particular the "social" insects such as termites and ants). Female chimpanzees tend to spend about twice as much of their time eating insects as do males.

Chimpanzees also occasionally hunt birds and small or young mammals such as deer, monkeys and bush pigs. Sometimes, they hunt alone. But animals such as monkeys are too fast and nimble for a chimpanzee working solo, so groups of two or more (usually male) often cooperate to hunt, thus greatly increasing their chances of making a kill.

When no fruit is available, chimpanzees substitute the pith from ground living plants. They usually get this from the stalks and stems of leafy plants such as Afromomum and Piper. Unlike fruit, pith is very low in sugar. It also has very little protein, but contains high levels of substances called cellulose and hemicellulose. These give structure to plant cell walls and are not particularly digestible.

However, thanks to their large stomachs and long guts, chimpanzees are quite efficient at digesting these high fibre foods.

In Kibale forest, Western Uganda, chimpanzees get most of their energy from pith when fruit is in short supply. Pith-eating increases when rainfall is high, possibly because that is when there are a lot of ground-living plants around.

FAMILY LIFE

FAMILY LIFE

When the young chimpanzee was only four, her mother died in a night nest. Initially, the orphan groomed her mother's body, but for the first time, the magic touch failed. Whimpering softly, she tugged at her mother's limp arms. When she gave up hope that her mother would ever again leave that tree, the youngster became listless and lost weight. She was found by one of her mother's close friends. The older female had lost two infants of her own. She had space and time in her life and adopted the little orphan. She shared her food with her adopted daughter, carried her, reassured her, and waited patiently for her so they could travel together.

When the older female had her own baby son, her adopted daughter became a doting older sister. Five years later, the old female died. However, her son was in safe hands. The orphan she had taken in all those years ago immediately took on responsibility for her foster brother's care.

Previous page: In a relaxed atmosphere, young chimpanzees practice locomotive skills that might, one day, save their life.

GROWING UP

A newborn chimpanzee weighs about 2 kg and is covered with jet-black hair, except for its wrinkled, pale pink face. It is helpless when it is born. The mother cups the baby in her hands and helps it reach her nipple to suckle. A few days later, the infant's grip of iron kicks in. It clings to its mother's belly hair with its feet and hands, hanging below her when they travel. As the infant grows bigger and stronger, it starts to wriggle around to get a better look at the world beyond its mother's body. Though still in near-constant physical contact with her, it starts to explore, popping its head out from under her armpit to reach for a stick, leaning back to scratch the earth, or stretching over her shoulder to fiddle with leaves or touch another chimpanzee. At six months, the baby pulls itself up for its first steps. By now it is growing too big to fit snugly under the mother's belly when she is traveling. It is time to move up in the world, onto her back. The young chimpanzee also learns about social life from watching how its mother behaves with other chimpanzees. For a few months, its mother provides everything it needs, food, comfort, warmth, a playmate, and security. However, there is a nasty shock in store.

From about five months old, a young chimpanzee starts to pay close attention to its mother's feeding habits, peering closely at her

1. Young chimpanzees depend on their parents for several years. A young chimpanzee has so many physical and social skills to master that growing up cannot be hurried.

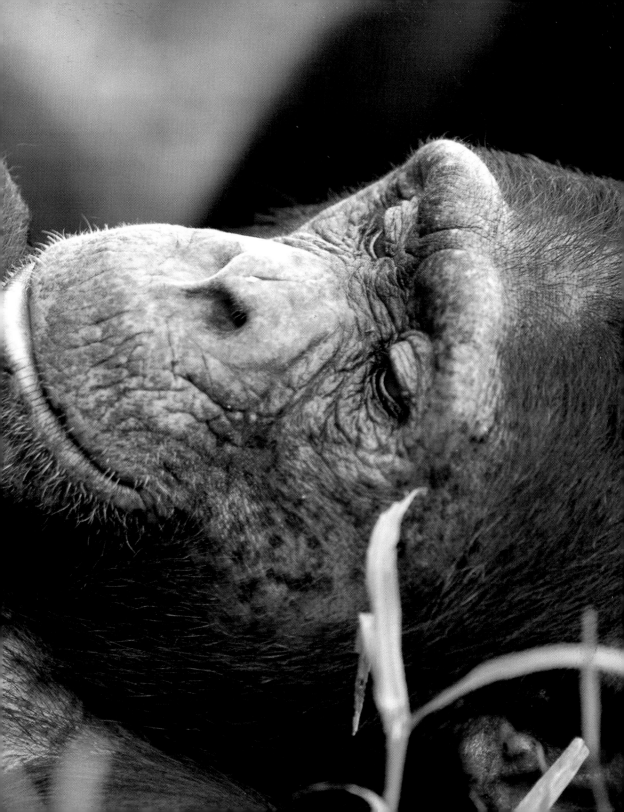

Previous page:
The powerful mother-infant emotional bond lasts way beyond the early years of dependency. Juveniles, adolescents, and even fully mature chimpanzees, will whimper if they cannot find their mothers.

mouth to get a good look at what she is eating. Between four and six months of age, the youngster chews food that its mother is eating, sometimes taking food from her hand. Over the next few months, it increasingly forages for itself, returning regularly to suckle. However, when it is between three and a half and four and a half years old, its mother starts to wean it off her milk. At first, if the infant pesters her enough, she will give in, but eventually she will refuse. This can send an infant into a frenzy, screaming and attacking its mother in an attempt to get to her nipple. The mother does her best to console and reassure her infant by hugging and grooming. She will sometimes try to distract it by tickling it. Between temper tantrums, the youngster becomes utterly miserable. It plays less

and sometimes sinks into listlessness and depression. This process can last for several weeks, sometimes even for months.

At about the same time, the mother launches another campaign, to get the youngster to travel on its own instead of riding on her back. Again, grooming fills the gap a little. Once this stage is over, the young chimpanzee plunges headlong into the next phase of its life.

Play and practice

Like the young of all social animals, young chimpanzees have an important job to do, play hard. Play helps them learn about their own bodies and what they can or can't do—how to handle the environment, and how to get along with other chimpanzees. Through adventure and fun, they figure out what the limits and the dangers are, and they practice preparing for and coping with the unexpected.

Sometimes they play alone. A young chimpanzee will, for example, spin around and around on its knuckles and heels, eyes shut, making itself dizzy. Young chimpanzees' energy seems never to run out. They are forever leaping around in small trees, hanging by one arm from the branches before crashing to the ground, just to repeat the whole sequence again. Or they play with things: tasting, biting, and nibbling; stamping in dust to make it fly up; wildly sweeping leaves up into piles and draping them over their shoulders; and pushing or dragging stones and sticks around.

When they are really enjoying themselves, for example, when another animal is tickling them, chimpanzees make a deep, throaty panting sound.

1. Mothers allow infants up to the age of three years old to take food from their hands or mouths.

2. The three characteristics of play are repetition, exaggeration, and restraint. Play, here, play-fighting, between youngsters helps forge lifelong friendships.

2

Learning Resources Center
Jordan High School
Jordan, Minnesota

Young chimpanzees will play together, too, and often their games can be sophisticated. Tickling, wrestling, somersaulting, chasing, and romping. The variations are endless. These games teach young chimpanzees about getting along with each other, restraint, and social rules. An older and bigger chimpanzee, for example, has to learn not to play too roughly and not to bite too hard.

Young chimpanzees have a little flag of white hair sticking up above their bottom. This is thought to be a visual signal to older chimpanzees, reminding them to respond to the youngster appropriately. Even the alpha male will tolerate lively youngsters bouncing off his body.

To get another chimpanzee to play with it, a youngster will often use what is known as a "play

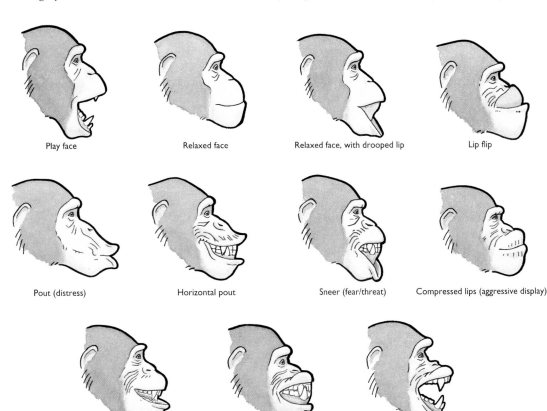

Play face   Relaxed face   Relaxed face, with drooped lip   Lip flip

Pout (distress)   Horizontal pout   Sneer (fear/threat)   Compressed lips (aggressive display)

1   Low closed grin (fear/excitement)   Full closed grin   Full open grin

hit," a special gesture that invites play. A juvenile will lift its arm and gently wallop a playmate to start a chase. Over time, the gesture becomes ritualized, so that all the chimpanzee has to do to initiate play is raise its arm high above its head, without actually hitting its playmate. Scientists think that these play gestures indicate that chimpanzees are aware of the recipient's role in the communication which is one of the signs of intelligence.

When chimpanzees play, they use a "play face," an expression to shows other chimpanzees that they are fighting in fun and that they mean no harm. The play face looks like a great big grin, but the chimpanzees cover their top teeth with their upper lips. If they did not, and their big teeth were bared, a play face could be misinterpreted as an aggressive facial

2

1. The chimpanzee's facial expressions, signaling a range of behaviors, include the full play face, which looks like a grin.

2. Young chimpanzees share characteristics with human children, including an aversion to boredom. Anything can be used as a plaything.

 LOOKS FAMILIAR

According to recent research, it appears that chimpanzees can spot family resemblances among others. However, it seems that, to a chimpanzee, males look more like their mothers than females do. When captive chimpanzees at the Yerkes Primate Research Center, in Atlanta, were shown photos of unfamiliar chimpanzees, they accurately matched females with their sons, but were not good at linking mothers and daughters. Perhaps it is more important to be "tuned into" male faces than female faces. Males, especially related males, often form alliances with each other during power struggles, so they need to know who is related to whom.

expression, and playtime could turn into a fight.

Along with trial and error, much learning happens by copying other chimpanzees. An infant will play with leaves and twigs while its mother uses a long stem to fish for termites. The infant will not catch any termites, but over time it learns how to pick the right stick, how to poke it into a termite hole, how to wiggle it around to make the termites bite, and how to slide it out without losing the insects. By the time it is four or five years old, a chimpanzee will become a skilled termite fisher.

Role models

Social behavior, too, is picked up by careful observation and role models. Jane Goodall, Director of the chimpanzee research station in the Gombe National Park, in Tanzania, tells two stories of a young male called Frodo. Once, Frodo watched carefully as his brother and hero, adolescent Freud, performed an impressive buttress-drumming display. Frodo, barely nine months old and still unstable on his feet, tried to do the same. He lost his balance, fell over, and had to be picked up by his mother. Later, when he was still young, he would try out fierce little displays on baboons, stomping and waving his arms around. If the baboons got irritated and aggressive, he would have to be rescued.

Older siblings often help with childcare. At Gombe, five-year-old Fifi was apparently captivated by her new baby brother, Flint. She played with him, groomed and carried him, and even protected him against others, helping mother Flo retrieve him from tricky situations. A first born has only its mother as playmate for some time, which can be isolating, especially if she is unsociable. Having an older sibling to play with improves the social skills of both, and some, though not all, siblings maintain strong bonds throughout their lives.

Adolescence

Young females get their first tiny genital swelling at 8 to 10 years old. This indicates that they have reached sexual maturity, though they are not actually fertile. Only at age 13 to 14 will this swelling, by then a grapefruit-sized pad of pink flesh, be an indication that a female is fertile. The "pinkness" makes the young female a magnet for males. After 10 days, the swelling deflates, as does the interest.

Males are sexually precocious, practicing intercourse on any pink females who will let them from the age of only two. Then, at about the age of seven, the young male must begin systematically challenging and dominating other chimpanzees.

1. Individual chimpanzees vary in how good they are at selecting and using tools for termite fishing.

2. Young orphans in a sanctuary play together. Most chimpanzees arrive in sanctuaries traumatized, having been caught in the wild and kept in appalling conditions.

2

MOTHERHOOD

To maximize her reproductive fitness, that is, to get as many of her genes as possible into future generations, a female's best bet, once she has conceived, is to make sure she takes good care of her offspring. If they make it to adulthood, her genes are more likely to make it to the next generation. For chimpanzees, being a good mother (males have little to do with rearing) requires a wide range of skills. Many of these are learned by watching other mothers. Hand-raised animals in zoos often make bad mothers because they have not had a chance to see first hand how it is done.

One Gombe female had no idea how to handle her first infant. She threw it over her back, picked it up by the leg, and let its head bump along the ground. She tucked it into her "pants pocket," the nook between a chimpanzee's thigh and its belly where food is sometimes carried. The baby died within a week. Her next baby survived, though its treatment was not much better. The mother seemed unable to understand the meaning of its whimpering and screams and kept leaving it behind. By the time the third infant arrived, she had managed to figure out mothering. Had she missed out in her early years on chances to handle infants?

A strong bond

The moment her baby is born, a female licks it clean and grooms it. The birth of an infant attracts huge interest from all the other chimpanzees. Adult males often cannot resist initiating play with an

1. Being a good mother requires a variety of skills many of which are learned by watching other chimpanzees.

2. A young chimpanzee learns to travel alone and be independent.

3. Grooming is a powerful social-bonding activity, which is why it often lasts much longer than would be necessary for hygiene.

3

older infant or scooping it up into a gentle hug. However, it is the females, in particular, who cannot keep away. They approach the mother, maybe grooming her in return for being allowed to look at or touch the new baby. Reluctant to let any other chimpanzees too close, the new mother often tries to keep them away, sometimes staying close to adult males for protection.

As the weeks pass, the mother increasingly lets those she trusts, an elder daughter, for example, get closer to her baby. Later, she allows her infant more freedom in moving away and interacting with others. The mother-infant bond, strong from the moment of birth, gets stronger, and creates an emotional dependency that is crucial for survival. The mother provides food, fun, company, warmth, protection, guidance, help, and a role model, for example, in terms of learning what can be eaten or how to interact socially with others. Whenever her youngster is upset or hurt, it immediately comes to

2

1. (opposite) Mothers carefully regulate access to their babies, but other chimpanzees may feign interest in something else in order to sidle close.

2. By the time Gombe chimpanzee Fifi gave birth to Ferdinand, her sixth baby, she knew exactly what to do.

 A TALE OF TWO MOTHERS

Jane Goodall watched two mothers at Gombe National Park bring up their daughters differently. Flo was highly sociable and spent hours playing with Fifi, her third infant. Passion preferred to spend her time alone. She rarely played with Pom, her first infant, and Pom became anxious and clinging. When it came to weaning, it seemed that though Fifi was affected, she quickly returned to her normal, playful self. Pom, on the other hand, showed signs of depression that lasted for months. Fifi spent hours playing with her younger brother, whereas Pom, interested in Passion's second infant at first, soon lost interest and appeared depressed again. At adolescence, Fifi, seen below as an adult with her own offspring, was calm and relaxed with males. Pom appeared nervous and tense. Observing these different styles of mothering, Jane Goodall became convinced that a chimpanzee's early experiences have a profound effect on its later behavior.

her for reassurance and comfort. A mother's soothing grooming can calm her off-spring as nothing else can. She grooms her infant for longer as it grows older, often to the youngster's dismay as it struggles to get free to go and play with its friends.

The mother-child bond lasts way beyond childhood. Even grown males, for example, suffering blows to their body or confidence in a fight seek comfort in their mother's arms.

Keeping careful watch

More than anything, being a good mother is about anticipating danger. Her youngster does not yet know its own physical limits or its community's social boundaries, and blunders can be dangerous. If the infant wanders over to an adult male, for example, and starts playing, she will scrutinize the male's expression and body language, ready to spring over and pluck her youngster away if the male shows signs of irritation. If play with another youngster gets too rough, she will put a stop to it before her baby gets hurt.

Young chimpanzees sometimes wrestle playfully with young baboons, often screaming loudly, and a chimpanzee mother may find herself face to face with an angry baboon mother. She may have to be aggressive to the baboon mother to get her to leave the young chimpanzee alone.

If a mother cannot see her baby, its scream will summon her in a flash to save it from a snake or from attack or intimidation.

The patience of some chimpanzee mothers never seems to run out. They will allow their infants to climb all over them, or they will sit and wait for ages while their youngster finishes its game or foraging. Other females are less tolerant, responding aggressively to rough play or dragging their infant away by the wrist. A three year old will be allowed to suckle, ride on its mother's back, and share her

PERSONALITY CRISIS

When the young Jane Goodall first went to Gombe, she gave the wild chimpanzees names. To the scorn of some other scientists, she also described the chimpanzees with words such as "adolescent," "child," "confident," "heartbroken," "shy," and "mischievous." At the time, it was not acceptable to assign these anthropomorphic "personality" traits to wild animals. Things have changed since then. Today, referring to chimpanzees' person-ality traits is not just acceptable, some fieldworkers say that it is essential. Granted, personality, that complex product of genetics, life history, and social background, is difficult to pin down scientifically, but there is no denying its power to affect behavioral choices and social interactions.

1. Each chimpanzee has its own web of social contacts. For young males, childhood playmates may, years later, become either staunch supporters or bitter rivals.

food, but over the next year or so, her tolerance begins to run out and she encourages her youngster to be more independent. Increasingly, she insists that it walks and feeds farther away from her. She reprimands it with mild aggression if it misbehaves, making it clear what is acceptable and what is not. However, grudges are never held, and chimpanzee mothers always offer reassurance and comfort immediately after discipline.

Adoption

If a young chimpanzee is orphaned, it may be adopted by an older brother or sister. When four-year-old Gombe chimpanzee Pax lost his mother, his older siblings tried to care for him. Though depressed, Pax gradually accepted the care his big brother, seven-year-old Prof, was trying to give him.

A year after their mother's death, Prof did many of the things that a mother would do. He waited for Pax when they were traveling together, searched for him if they got separated and generally stuck by him. Once, after he had examined Pax's running nose, Prof wiped the snot away with a fistful of leaves. Another time, Pax threw a temper tantrum, and the noise made the alpha male nearby angry. He glowered at the youngster, his hair bristling. Sensing danger like a good mother would, Prof rushed over to his troublesome brother and dragged him away.

Occasionally, something unusual happens, an unrelated chimpanzee adopts the orphan. When three-year-old Mel lost his mother, there were no relatives to take him in. It seemed unlikely that the increasingly sickly youngster would survive. Then, to the astonishment of the Gombe fieldworkers, a totally unrelated adolescent male called Spindle struck up a relationship with Mel. The two shared night nests, and Spindle protected Mel as best he could from the older males, even letting Mel climb onto his back to travel.

Sons or daughters?

Chimpanzees have the same number of sons and daughters on average, but at Taï Forest National Park mothers "choose" (in evolutionary terms) to invest more time and energy in one sex or the other. The way they do this is by varying the so-called inter-birth interval, the time before they have another baby. Young chimpanzees benefit greatly from an extra few months of undivided care and attention, and the inter-birth interval has a strong effect on the first-born's chances of survival. If her baby is the preferred sex, the mother will wait longer before having the next.

For a mother, a son is a high-risk, high-gain bet. He could provide her with a great many grand-children, but he could also fail completely and not father a single baby. A daughter is a much safer bet: unless she is sterile, she is sure to produce at least one child. But a daughter could never reach the dizzy heights of reproductive success that a son might achieve.

So which to favor, sons or daughters? The deciding factor appears to be rank. High-ranking females can back up their offspring and help them to do well. For high-ranking mothers, it is worth putting that extra effort into sons. With sons, high-ranking females wait, on average, 26 months longer before having another baby than if a daughter is

1. An infant's first experience of play is its mother's gentle nibbling and tickling.

1

born. The extra two years of undivided mothering gives them a better survival rate: 30 percent more sons of dominant females at Taï reach adulthood than those of subordinate females. High-ranking mothers at Taï are also more involved than low-ranking females in their sons' careers. The males Kendo, Fitz and Snoopy, sons of high-ranking Ella and Salomé, all progressed rapidly in the hierarchy. Low-ranking females contribute little to their sons' social standing. For these mothers, it makes more sense to concentrate on daughters. Subordinate females invest on average 12 months more in daughters than in sons.

But these patterns are not the same in all chimpanzee societies. At Gombe, high-ranking females have a shorter inter-birth interval than low-ranking ones, but there is no difference in relation to gender. This may be because at Gombe only a few young females transfer to other groups, so high-ranking mothers with daughters get compensation in terms of continuing support and affiliation. At Taï, most daughters leave home, and there is not much opportunity for lifelong bonds.

Borrowed rank

Chimpanzees, particularly males, have to work for their position in the community, but a youngster's ability to establish his dominance is influenced by his mother's behavior. The offspring of high-ranking females see others deferring to her and they, too, will be treated with more respect when she is

1. Bristling is a clear indication of high levels of arousal, either excitement or, in this case, aggression. A bristling male is likely to display or attack.

2. Researchers at Gombe charted the rise and fall in social rank between 1963 and 1983 of a number of male chimpanzees who attempted to achieve alpha status.

THE RISE AND FALL OF GOMBE MALES

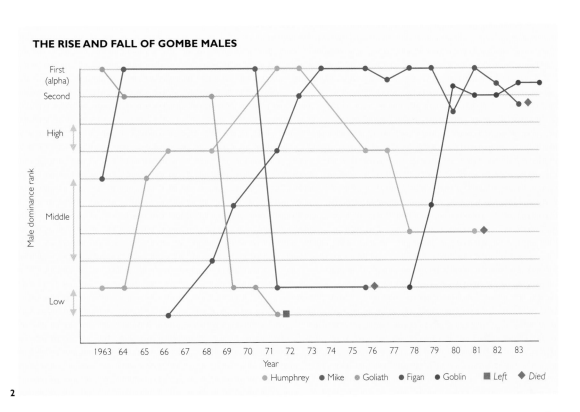

Male dominance rank

First (alpha) / Second / High / Middle / Low

Year
1963 64 65 66 67 68 69 70 71 72 73 74 75 76 77 78 79 80 81 82 83

● Humphrey ● Mike ● Goliath ● Figan ● Goblin ■ Left ◆ Died

2

around. Young males with dominant mothers will challenge older females sooner and with more daring when their mother is around to back them up. If they follow this advantage through with strong personality traits of their own, determination and sociability, for example, they are more likely to make it to the top. So a mother's rank clearly shapes a young chimpanzee's future behavior.

From an early age, a young male will start to bristle and swagger in order to intimidate and dominate females. If his mother is high-ranking, she will back him up. When he is older and bigger, he can return the favor. As time goes by, the company of his mother and younger siblings becomes less interesting to a young adolescent male. Older males, though, become absolutely fascinating to him. When they are near and relaxed, he ventures closer to take part in grooming sessions. However, a male will not be fully integrated into the social hierarchy until he is between 13 and 16 years old.

POWER AND SEX

3   POWER AND SEX

The first sign of trouble was when the young adult male, his friend and protégé for so many years, did not rush to greet the old alpha male as usual. It was a small thing, but full of implied threat. Shaken, the alpha male sought reassurance from his inner court of four loyal males. Later, the challenges started. The young male's favorite trick was surprise, and he had learned that from the alpha. He would wake the other chimpanzees with sudden violent displays right above their nests, or jump out from his hiding place in the undergrowth. When they had their first serious fight, the young male kicked the alpha out of a tree.

For the next five months, the top job was vacant. The alpha, his confidence wrecked, could not claim it any more, but together he and his friends easily dominated the young one. Eventually they all succumbed to the younger male and the old alpha disappeared for good.

Previous page: Chimpanzee social life involves plenty of physical contact. For common chimpanzees, this means lots of grooming, hugging, and kissing. For bonobos, it also includes sexual contact that is not reproductive, such as between these two infants.

ALPHA AND BELOW

In most primates, one male defends a harem of related females. However, because of the way chimpanzees forage, travel in small groups, it is impossible for a male to single-handedly defend all his females. Instead, a core group of possibly related males defends a large territory and the females that live there together. However, below the cooperative surface lies fiercely competitive individuals. Their key to reproductive success is a high placing in the dominance rank. The ranking system is strict, but fluid. At the top is the alpha male. Below him is a secondary rank, often occupied by a recently toppled alpha or an up-and-coming younger male. Relations between the alpha and the second-in-command tend to be tense. Then come the lower echelons of subordinate males, females, juveniles, and infants.

It can take many years and a lot of hard work to get to the top. The alpha will have had to challenge every single adult male ranked above him. Overtaking a male one position ahead can take weeks, sometimes months, of effort. At some point he will have had to topple the previous alpha. However, the rewards are worth striving for. Along with front-row feeding rights and total respect from all the other chimpanzees in the community, the alpha male has the first choice when it comes to fertile females. To reserve these privileges he must maintain order, keep the peace, ensure that he is being given respect, and thwart the ambitions of other males.

1. Though he is usually a male in his prime, the alpha male is not necessarily the most physically powerful in the community. Highly developed social skills and strong personal qualities are equally important.

STRONG FRIENDS

Best of friends or most bitter of rivals, their intensity characterizes relationships between adult male chimpanzees. They fight more than the females do, groom more, about four times as much as females, cooperate more, make more noise, and spend many more relaxed hours together. Males "kiss" 20 times as much as females, and one study showed that 80 percent of hugs are between males. If a large group of chimpanzees gathers at a large fruit tree, a high-ranking male will display vigorously, creating bedlam. It is his way of finding out quickly if there have been any crucial changes in rank. Low rankers fall over themselves to reassure him of the status quo.

To edge into this close-knit fellowship, a young male will sometimes shadow an older one he admires, perhaps a brother, following him and grooming him. He will also need allies. Together, two chimpanzees can stand up to a third that neither of them would have dared stand up to alone. A chimpanzee's success at recruiting support depends on his social skills, his temperament, and on how good he is at paying back favors.

Until recently, it was believed that in multi-male chimpanzee society, the strongest social bonds were between males, with females remaining aloof. The evidence for this comes from the Tanzanian chimpanzee societies at Mahale and Gombe. However, it now appears that Taï females enjoy a rich social life, and that bonds between females are at least as strong as those between males. "The view of chimpanzees as a purely male-oriented society does not reflect the social life in Taï chimpanzees," report primatologists Christophe Boesch and Hedwige Boesch-Achermann. "Taï females build strong

1. Most grooming happens between individuals who already have, or want to have, a close relationship.

2. Together, two males, here, Yeroen and Nikkie, can stand up to a third that neither would dare stand up to alone.

friendships and alliances with other females, are active grooming partners, take an active role in the social conflicts between the males, and make coalitions with some of them."

At Mahale and Gombe, females almost never attack males, nor are they involved in confrontations between males. The contrast with Taï is striking—seventeen attacks involving female coalitions against males and four joint-sex attacks were seen there in two months.

Researchers suggest that the tropical rain forest environment is responsible for these marked social differences. There are greater opportunities for females to mix, and in this rich environment chimpanzees can live in much bigger groups, which sets the scene for greater sociability and a bisexually bonded society.

Power struggles

Most of the time, males indulge in elaborate rituals in which they go out of their way to acknowledge, rather than challenge, each other's rank. However, if a subordinate fails to show immediate deference in the presence of the alpha male, things can get noisy.

The triangular power struggle between male chimpanzees at Arnhem Zoo in the Netherlands was so extraordinary that, in the United States, Frans de Waal's book *Chimpanzee Politics* became recommended reading for new members of Congress. The social tactics of three male chimpanzees, Yeroen, Nikkie, and Luit, proved that political manipulation is not solely confined to human beings.

2

Female chimpanzees sometimes intervene in conflicts. They may quietly remove a stone from a male's hand if he is about to throw it.

It all began when young Luit began to challenge the old alpha, Yeroen. Luit would systematically try to break up any grooming groups that Yeroen was involved in. Over several months, Yeroen spent less and less time with his potential supporters, and Luit eventually rose to the top. Once there, he tried to prevent the defeated alpha from spending time with another male, Nikkie. This time, though, Luit's divide-and-conquer strategy did not work. Yeroen and Nikkie still managed to form a coalition so strong that Nikkie, supported by Yeroen, defeated Luit.

Nikkie's position at the top was precarious. He relied on Yeroen to back him in his interactions with other chimpanzees. Yeroen, in turn, did not stop at supporting Nikkie. He also spent a lot of energy preventing Nikkie and Luit from ganging up against him. It all ended in one violent, unobserved, nighttime showdown. Luit's battered body was found later, his scrotum and one leg torn right off.

Real brothers

Of all the allies a chimpanzee can have, a brother is the most valuable. Gombe chimpanzee Figan owed his alpha position to his older brother, Faben. When they were young, Figan supported Faben in his challenges to other chimpanzees. Then Faben suffered a tragedy. An illness left one of his arms paralyzed. Figan wasted no time in exploiting his brother's weakness and dominating him. For the next three years, the only time the brothers spent together was when they both joined their mother.

Figan continued to challenge low-ranking chimpanzees. Just ahead of him was another young

4

1–3. At Gombe, Goblin grooms alpha male Figan (1). Figan brushes a fly away and Goblin, thinking the gesture was a threat, leaps back, screaming (2). He then seeks reassurance (3).

4. The alpha male's stiff-shouldered, hunched, pinched-lipped, scowling charge leaves other chimpanzees in no doubt of his superiority. It is a terrifying performance.

male, and an old playmate, Evered. For several months, Figan and Evered challenged each other. With chimpanzees of different ranks, a hunched-up, bristled-up, stand-up swagger from the more dominant one usually does the trick. These two, though, were so closely matched that challenges frequently turned over into full-scale charges and fights. Evered was older, and he usually won. Then, when Figan was 16, Faben's attitude changed. Occasionally he began to back up his younger brother. The first time this happened, the brothers teamed up to challenge Evered, and it was a walkover.

Later, the brothers' status in society suddenly moved up a notch because of a change at the top. The elderly, balding, worn-out alpha, Mike, was suddenly and decisively overthrown by a powerful and aggressive male, Humphrey. "It marked the end of an era, Mike's six-year reign as alpha," says Jane Goodall. "Almost overnight, he became one of the lowest-ranking males of his community. Even some of the adolescents began to challenge him, and Mike seldom tried to stand up for himself."

The new alpha, Humphrey, enlisted Evered to back up his position, but his reign was short lived. Again, it was Faben who facilitated this next social earthquake. From supporting Figan once in a while, or at least, not joining sides against him, Faben seemed to pledge absolute commitment to helping his brother in his bid for the top. If Figan challenged another male, Faben was by his side. With Faben backing him, Figan ousted Humphrey from the number one spot.

BEHAVIORS AFTER AN ATTACK

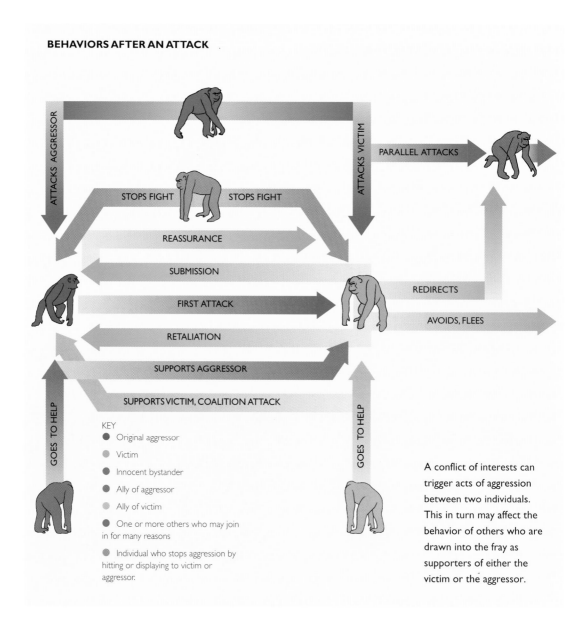

KEY
- Original aggressor
- Victim
- Innocent bystander
- Ally of aggressor
- Ally of victim
- One or more others who may join in for many reasons
- Individual who stops aggression by hitting or displaying to victim or aggressor.

A conflict of interests can trigger acts of aggression between two individuals. This in turn may affect the behavior of others who are drawn into the fray as supporters of either the victim or the aggressor.

MALE SEXUAL STRATEGIES

There is nothing like a big, pink bottom to focus the attention of every male. Unless she is pregnant or suckling an infant, an adult female's perineal skin swells up like a balloon when she is sexually receptive. She is fertile for a few days, and it is in every adult male's interest to be the one that gets her pregnant.

Many of the female chimpanzees wandering around the home range could become fertile at any time. Males need to be there when they do. Should a male search the home range and hope to bump into several females? It is risky. He may not meet any, or they may have been fertilized already by other males. Or should he go for a low-risk, low-return strategy and pick a female to stick by until she becomes fertile? There would be only one infant, but at least it would be his.

The final battle to father an infant takes place on an intimate level. Sperm from different males compete within the female's reproductive tract. The more sperm a male can ejaculate, the higher his chances of fertilizing the egg. Sperm competition goes further, because there is a coagulant in primate semen. The semen forms a plug at the entrance to the female's vagina in an attempt to prevent other sperm getting through.

Courtship

Before he can mate, a male must first court a female. He indicates his desire by sitting and gazing straight at the female, legs wide apart, his genitals on display.

1

1. Her tempting sexual swelling advertises a female's fertility.

2. It is tough at the top. The alpha must be constantly on the alert for trouble.

2

★ Chimpanzee sex takes six or seven seconds: 10 times quicker than gorillas, who take about a minute, and 100 times quicker than orang-utans, who mate for about 11 minutes.

He may add other gestures like shaking a nearby branch, reaching out toward her, or bristling his hair up. Sometimes, he will knock the ground with his knuckles, stamp his foot, or stand up and swagger. The female responds by approaching him and presenting her rear. Mating lasts a few seconds and is noisy. He pants, and she squeals. A dozen or so males may mate with a single female in quick succession. At first, this male tolerance seems odd, given how much power an alpha could exert.

1

However, males must work together to protect the territory, and access to females is the reward for that cooperation. Males can afford to be tolerant of each other and there are other paths to fatherhood. The alpha steps in when it matters. A female's swelling reaches its maximum when she is about to ovulate. Then the chances of conception soar. Males seem to be able to tell roughly when this happens, possibly from changes in the odor of the female's vaginal secretions, as well as the size of her swelling.

1. The males of some primate species kill infants they know are not theirs. By mating with many different males, female chimpanzees keep the paternity of their offspring hidden, therefore reducing the risk of infanticide.

Now, the alpha male pulls rank and escorts her everywhere. His presence is enough to dissuade other males from trying to mate with her.

Consortship

Lower-ranking males cannot monopolize a female at the crucial time in this way. The chances of fertilizing her early in her swelling, with all the other males doing the same, are low. The best bet is to be alone with her. Therefore a male will try to form a special relationship with one female, a short-term, monogamous relationship known as a consortship.

First, he must lure her away. The best time to do this is early on in her swelling, before she is surrounded by other attentive males. He uses the usual courtship signals, but this time, when she approaches, he gets up and moves away, looking over his shoulder to check that she is following. If she is not, he will start again. If she is still reluctant, his displays may become more vigorous and erupt into a full-scale charge.

If his beckoning works, he leads her rapidly away. Once out of earshot, they both relax. There are no other chimpanzees around, and the female is now so far from others that she really has no choice but to stick to her consort for safety. They groom each other frequently.

Consortships can last from a few hours to a few weeks. If he can keep her by his side for the whole of her swelling, or even an entire cycle, the male has a good chance of fathering an infant. However, he does put himself out of the competition for other females that become fertile.

FEMALE SEXUAL STRATEGIES

A female has the same goal as a male, to usher as many of her genes as she can safely into future generations. Chimpanzee females, who have a single infant at a time, do not have many chances to reproduce since their offspring have long childhoods. A female who has five infants is doing well, and at Gombe, Fifi's eight babies, only one of whom died, represent an amazing reproductive success. Each infant is a huge investment for a chimpanzee female. Once it is born, she must devote all her time and effort to ensuring that she can nourish and care for it until it can look after itself. As a result, female chimpanzees are much more concerned with being good parents than male chimpanzees. The key to their own genetic success lies in ensuring that each infant survives to adulthood, not with attempting as many matings as possible.

However, what about before an infant is born? Half of an individual's genes come from its father. A female can influence her child's genetic future enormously by ensuring that it gets a top-quality father. That way she can siphon off some of his characteristics, good health, strength, size, and attractiveness, for her child.

With all those noisy, aggressive males fighting over her when she is pink, summoning her over to mate or marching her off on a long consortship, it might appear that a female chimpanzee has little say in who makes her pregnant. However, there are several things she can do to exert some choice.

Early on in her swelling, a female cooperates with all the males who want to mate. Later, when her

1

2

3

1–6. Female chimpanzees will often mate with two or more males in quick succession, especially at times of food excitement, such as when bananas were provided at Gombe. In this sequence, Leakey, his

mouth stuffed with bananas, raises his arm to invite Gigi to mate (1). Goliath approaches (2–3), and Gigi then mates with him, too (4–5), before escaping up the tree (6).

swelling is at its peak, the female gets choosy. Now, at ovulation, when she is at her most fertile, she reserves her favors for one or two top males, one of whom will probably be the father.

Just say no – or go!

At Gombe, where there are as many males as females, males are more likely to impose their will on females. At Taï, though, there are three times more females than males, and females form stronger coalitions. Females have much more social power and are much better able to resist male pressure to mate. Some males are of course easier to ignore than others. Saying no to the alpha is not an option. Refusing lower-ranking males is easier.

Because male chimpanzees stay in the community they are born in, they are likely to be related. It is the females who move out in order to side-step the risk of inbreeding. Some females leave home for good. This is best done when they are young and sexually attractive, which ensures a warm welcome from the neighboring males, though resident females are not too pleased at this competition for resources. A female makes a few visits to her new chosen community while still living in her own, and so it can take some time for her to move away for good. She usually commits to a community during her first pregnancy. Some females just nip over the border to collect some good-quality sperm and then come home again, and local males are none the wiser. Some 13 percent of conceptions seen at Gombe resulted from matings with males from other communities.

BONOBOS: SEX FOR EVERYTHING

Sex, for all non-human animals, is about repro-
ducing, unless you are a bonobo, in which case sex
is also about greeting, playing, dominating, peace-
keeping, sharing, negotiating, comforting, relaxing,
and just having fun. Sex occurs between every
possible combination of partners and in many
different positions. Bonobos are, without doubt,
seriously keen on sex.

No other primate has sex so frequently. In
bonobos, sex is a social tool, replacing grooming as
the glue that binds animals together. If there is
disagreement, it is resolved with sex; if there is
aggression, it is cooled with sex. If two bonobos
haven't seen each other for a while, they greet with
sex; if they want something, it is traded for sex.

Sisterhoods

Information about bonobos is accumulating. One
thing is clear: solidarity between unrelated females
is the cornerstone of bonobo community. Working
together, they form "sisterhoods" through which
they dominate males – or at least, stop males from
dominating them. Male bonobos are not nearly as
bothered by status or politics as common
chimpanzees are, although the alpha male position
is fiercely fought for.

Sons of high-ranking mothers tend to make it to
the top. Sons of low-ranking females fare badly. At
the Wamba research site, the highest ranking
female was Kame. Of her three sons, the eldest, Ibo,
was alpha male. Another young male, Ten, started
to challenge the sons, though he was always beaten

1. Juveniles practice their
sexual-social skills through
genito-genital (G-G)
rubbing from an early age.

2. Bonobos have a far
richer array of vocal-
izations, facial expressions,
and gestures linked to
sexual activity than
common chimpanzees.

2

by Ibo. Things changed when Ten's strong, fit mother got involved. First, she defeated Ibo herself, alone, in a serious fight. Then she challenged the brothers' mother, old Kame, and beat her, too. Kame lost her alpha-female position. After his mother's defeat, Ibo, too, became submissive and lost his alpha position to Ten. After old Kame died, her sons' ranks slipped further.

Usually, aggression is limited to minor acts such as biting to get food. When groups meet on the edges of their home range, they might let out a few warning calls, but there is rarely any physical violence. All in all, bonobos prefer to settle conflicts of interest without violence.

☆ Bonobos sometimes mark out personal space during the day, for resting, grooming, or play, by making a "taboo nest" on the ground. No other bonobo will enter without invitation.

WILD INTELLIGENCE

WILD INTELLIGENCE

The Guinea chimpanzees had never seen anything like it. There were plenty of oil-palm nuts in the forest, and the chimpanzees knew how to get the kernels, choose a stone, put the almond-shaped nut on one of the unmovable stone anvils, raise the hammer, and crack! However, these nuts were different. They were round and covered in a thick rind that was impossible to bite open. Then Yo, a 31-year-old female, came over. She took a pile of the new coula nuts to an anvil and cracked them open, while the juveniles watched.

Two days later, a six-year-old male, without any practice, cracked a coula nut open and spat it out. A young female did the same, and soon they both got a taste for the new nuts. When the researchers stopped providing "strange" coula nuts after a fortnight, Yo probably missed them. She was not originally from Guinea but migrated from Sierra Leone 22 miles over the border. She had cracked coula nuts there too.

Previous page: Chimpanzees are the only nonhuman animals that make and adapt tools regularly in the wild. Here, a youngster sucks moisture from a moss-covered stick.

MANIPULATING THE ENVIRONMENT

A sea otter floats on its back, balances a mollusk shell on its belly, and cracks it open with a stone held between its paws. A Galapagos finch pokes for food in tree crevices with a cactus spine in its beak. An Egyptian vulture drops a stone to smash an ostrich egg. They are all using tools.

Though this behavior is fascinating because it is so rare, these animals are stuck in a rut. Their behavior is rigid because they always use the same tools in the same way. Chimpanzees are in a different league, because not only do they use several tools for different jobs, but they also make and adapt tools. They even use objects to solve new problems. They are smart enough to be flexible, to

experiment, to remember, to plan ahead, and to understand the relationship between different things. More importantly, tools give chimpanzees the edge when it comes to making the most out of their environment.

Cracking nuts

Many plants lock up their precious seeds in a home-grown safe, like a shell, tough skin, or a spiky capsule, to protect them from disease and hungry animals. In many areas, chimpanzees ignore nuts because they are so difficult to eat, but not in West Africa. There are five different types of nuts in the Taï Forest National Park. Researchers who studied the Taï chimpanzees for many years were the first to witness the chimpanzees' ingenious hammer-and-

1. In the nutting season in the Taï forest, nut-cracking "workshops" form. With the same hammer, the chimpanzees can switch from pounding to gentle taps, depending on how much force is needed.

1

anvil nut-cracking technique. The chimpanzees collect nuts and put them on an anvil, a large, unmovable stone or exposed tree root. Good anvils are rare, and so lines to use them sometimes form. Some of the nuts are harder than others and the chimpanzees carefully choose hammers weighing anywhere from 10 oz to 44 lb (280 g-20 kg). Then they hit the nut'sshell with just the right force to break it open. It is a difficult technique to master, and females motivate their youngsters by sharing the nuts that they have already cracked.

Using tools this way gives the Taï chimps a huge dietary bonus since at the height of the season this can amount to an average of 270 nuts, about 4000 calories, per day. When there are plenty of nuts around, chimpanzees will spend up to three hours a day cracking them. The stone anvils are worn smooth with constant use, and the ground is littered with empty shells.

Using tools and weapons

Termites, like other social insects such as bees and ants, live in colonies of thousands of insects. They build a rough pyramid of hardened mud that can be several yards high. The termites live inside, out of sight, in hollow chambers joined by passageways. Some chimpanzees get the termites out by "fishing" for them, a behavior first recorded by Jane Goodall in Gombe. Until then, it was thought that only humans used tools.

First, they choose a probe, which might be a stem, a twig, a vine, or a piece of grass. Picking the right tool comes with experience since it has to be just the right thickness, suppleness, and length. The chimpanzee strips off any leaves, pokes the end of the stem into one of the tunnels, waits, carefully slides the probe out keeping the insects on the stick, and finslly licks off the termites.

1. A tool is an object that an animal holds to achieve a short-term goal, such as feeding itself.

2. Props such as sticks, stones, branches, and occasionally water boost the impact of an aggressive display.

In the termite season, chimpanzees might use tools every day. They do not usually eat termites in the dry season because they are deeper in the mound and more difficult to catch. However, chimpanzees in the Congo's Ndoki Forest have solved this problem and can eat termites all year round. They do not use just one tool. They have a tool kit. They break open a clear passageway into the termite mound using a stout "perforating stick," then they switch tools and pick up a flexible stem as a probe.

To get driver ants, which live in underground nests, chimpanzees use another tool and technique. They break open the nest and dip a long, stiff stick, or "wand" into the mass of angry ants. When the ants have swarmed about halfway up, the chimpanzee wipes them off with a sweep through its hand and stuffs them into its mouth, chewing frantically to avoid their vicious bites.

If a chimpanzee cannot reach rainwater that has collected in a tree hollow with its lips, it will sometimes make a sponge of crumpled leaves, which it repeatedly dips into the water to soak it up. Chimpanzees will also use handfuls of leaves to wipe fruit juice, urine, blood, mud, mucus, semen, or feces off themselves.

Some of the differences in tool use between sites can be explained by the environment. If the raw materials do not exist in the first place, they cannot be used. In Gombe, there are lots of termites, and therefore fishing with probes is popular. There are plenty of nuts in Taï, which gives young chimpanzees opportunities to watch others cracking nuts and to practice themselves. There would be no point learning to crack nuts if there were none around.

2

☆ Some chimpanzees get around the lack of water by digging for large, water-filled roots, which they carry around and share, like a bottle.

2

1. (opposite) Tool use requires manual dexterity and an ability to "see" how an object might be used to achieve something.

2. Materials are usually modified before they can be used as tools, so chimpanzees must have a mental image of the final product and how to make it.

CULTURE

Some of the things that chimpanzee populations do differently cannot be accounted for by environmental factors. Zoologists use the term "culture" to talk about variations in the ways separate groups of the same species behave.

Behavior is transmitted in two ways. The first is genetically since animals are born with the ability to perform certain behaviors. This is called an instinct. Many young birds "imprint" the first image they see after they are hatched, usually their mother, and follow it faithfully thereafter. In fact, in captivity chicks can also become imprinted on humans and even inanimate objects, if they see them during the brief critical period after hatching. As with physical characteristics, this type of behavior is inherited and has been shaped by biological evolution.

Other forms of behavior are much more flexible and are learned by individuals during their lifetime, not inherited. If a behavior pattern is learned by many individuals and occurs throughout the population, it is recognized as cultural behavior since it develops and changes through cultural evolution and is spread through cultural transmission.

The sweet potato story is perhaps the most famous example of a behavior pattern spreading through a group by social means. Researchers threw sweet potatoes onto a beach for Japanese macaques to eat, which soon became covered in sand. One day, a female macaque did something none of the monkeys had ever done before. She carried her sweet potato to the sea and rinsed off the sand. The

Learning Resources Center
Jordan High School
Jordan, Minnesota

1

other animals watched this new trick, and it was not long before they were all washing their sweet potatoes. Today, food rinsing still happens, even though all the original macaques are dead. There are other examples in nature. For example, many songbirds pick up their native song-dialect by cultural learning. Among most species, only a single behavior is known to be transmitted culturally. Among chimpanzees, there are nearly 40.

Researchers have pooled information on cultural behavior from the seven long-term chimpanzee study sites, Gombe and Mahale in Tanzania, Budongo and Kibale in Uganda, Bossou in Guinea, and the Taï Forest in the Ivory Coast. Learned behaviors were compared across the different sites to see if there was cultural variation between the

different populations. Of the 65 behaviors that were examined as candidates for culture, 26 were discounted. In some of these, the variation could be explained by enviromental factors. For example, nests will not be built on the ground in areas where there are predators like lions or leopards. Other behaviors, including leaf sponges, branch shaking to attract attention, buttress drumming, and dragging branches during displays, occured everywhere. Some behaviors, like using a stick to step over thorns, or as a nostril cleaner, were not widespread enough anywhere to count.

That left 39 behaviors that could be counted as cultural variations. These are common in some communities but do not occur in others. There was as much variation within the two species of ▷▷

chimpanzee as between them, which means the differences in behavior have nothing to do with genetics. Many behaviors involved tool use, grooming and courtship, which is, both technology and social behavior. For example, at Taï, Mahale, and Kibale, the chimpanzees groom each other by holding hands high above their heads and grooming with their free hand. This is not seen elsewhere. Rain dances, which are displays triggered by storms, rushing wind, or water, occur everywhere except at Bossou. The chimpanzees at Gombe are the only ones to use an object to tickle themselves, but they are also the only ones that do not "leaf clip", where a male tries to get a female's attention by picking a stiff leaf, noisily biting it off, and spitting it out in small pieces. Only chimpanzees at Taï use a stick to scrape the marrow out of bones. At Budongo, they inspect parasites with a leaf, and at Gombe they use a leaf to flatten parasites. Kibale chimpanzees "leaf-dab," pat at wounds with leaves, the most.

These results took the researchers by surprise. They revealed a rich pattern of cultural variation that was far more extensive than had ever been documented in chimpanzees before. What scientists cannot agree on is how cultural transmission happens.

Learning

Animals figure out how to do some things all by themselves. They pick up other behaviors through various forms of social learning. A young chimpanzee picks up termite fishing by watching its mother. A juvenile male practices displays by copying the alpha male. A female's attention is drawn to an anvil by the nut shells scattered

1. Chimpanzees constantly use their high intelligence in their complex social lives, as well as to get the most out of their physical environment.

 ON REFLECTION

Monkeys react aggressively to their own mirror image. They never figure out that it is themselves that they see in the mirror. Chimpanzees and orangutans, on the other hand, realize after a few days that they are looking at themselves. In a classic experiment, Gordon Gallup demonstrated this when he put a spot of dye on the foreheads of chimpanzees accustomed to mirrors without them knowing. When the chimpanzees saw themselves in the mirror, they immediately touched the dye on their forehead. This has led many scientists to conclude that chimpanzees have a "concept of self," they understand who they are.

1. Tool-acquired food is rarely shared, so the situation at Taï, where mothers often share nuts with their infants, is unusual. The better the youngster gets at cracking, the fewer nuts it gets from its mother.

around it. A young chimpanzee, of its own accord, experiments, tastes, and plays with food. The mother will actively prevent it from trying to eat leaves from a poisonous plant, but is she teaching it? There is a lot of debate about this. For it to count as real teaching, the "teacher" must *intend* to teach. Observing and measuring "intention" in animals is impossible. The only solution is to watch and see if the "teacher" appears to evaluate how the learner is doing and modifies the "lesson" accordingly. This is extremely rare.

Among chimpanzees in the wild, the only examples come from the nut-cracking chimpanzees of Taï. Christophe Boesch tells a story about Ricci and her five-year-old daughter Nina. Ricci was cutting down the number of nuts she shared with Nina and instead gave her unopen nuts and hammers, which fit into Nina's

improving technical level. One day, Ricci was watching Nina, who was struggling to crack open a nut. Nina tried changing her grip on the hammer and then moved the nut around, but nothing worked. After 8 minutes, Ricci walked over to her daughter. "Nina immediately handed over the troublesome hammer," says Boesch. "Deliberately, Ricci slowly rotated it to the best position for nut cracking. As if to emphasize the significance of this movement, Ricci took a full minute to perform this simple rotation." Ricci, with Nina watching carefully, then opened 10 nuts, of which Nina ate six. When Nina took over the hammer again, she used the same grip her mother had demonstrated and opened a few nuts by herself. "Ricci's behavior is . . . the first clear case of teaching in any nonhuman animal in the wild," said Boesch.

TEAMWORK

Cooperation between chimpanzees is essential for hunting, and also to defend the community's territory against other chimpanzee groups. These activities put heavy demands on chimpanzees" mental abilities. They need to plan, think strategically, and predict the behavior of others.

Patrols

Territory is precious. As a community grows, it needs more resources, and cannot afford to let neighboring chimpanzees encroach too far. Therefore two or three times a week, a band of male chimpanzees, with fertile females tagging along, sets off to patrol the far reaches of the home range.

The chimpanzees' behavior on these patrols is different from that on normal travel. On patrol, they walk in a tight group, often in single file, appearing purposeful, tense, and cautious. They stop frequently to listen and look around, sometimes climbing a tree to look out over their neighbors' range. They stay silent and avoid stepping on dry leaves, and their hair bristles as they move deeper into unknown territory. Sudden sounds, even something as innocuous as a cracking twig, startle them, and they reach out, fear grinning, to touch or hug each other. Usually, patrols involve a few hours of checking for signs of intruders. The chimps will sniff at discarded fruit or tools, or inspect a fresh nest. Perhaps the smell of another chimpanzee can tell them about the stranger's sex and age. Home ranges frequently ▷▷

 TALKING APES

When, in the mid 1950s, researchers first tried to teach a chimpanzee to speak, they got no more than a few strangled sounds. Today, Kanzi, a captive bonobo (see below), says "Put the toothbrush in the lemonade," "Can you brush Liz's hair?" and "Hide the toy gorilla." The difference is that Kanzi points to symbols on a keyboard. Other chimpanzees have learned hundreds of words in sign language. In human toddlers, the larynx, or voice box, drops to allow speech. This does not happen in chimpanzees, therefore they are more successful at learning human language when speech production is not required. According to Kanzi's teacher, Sue Savage-Rumbaugh, Kanzi can understand more than 650 spoken sentences and produces sentences similar to those of a child of three and a half.

2

PANT HOOTS

Pant hoots are the chimpanzee's most common call. A pant hoot starts with a series of low hoots that build up to a deep roar or high-pitched scream. They can carry for more than 5 miles, and chimpanzees have different "voices." The calls are often accompanied by banging on buttresses, a low-frequency noise that also carries a long way. Males respond to two thirds of calls they hear with a pant hoot of their own, whereas females reply to only one third. Pant hoots seem to function in the same way as the howling of a wolf pack. It helps the animals keep in touch. The "roar" pant hoot is thought to be used to maintain contact between allies. On patrol, a group of males uses pant hoots to assess the size of a rival group. The "wail pant hoot" announces the discovery of a supply of food and the more food, the more pant hoots.

1. (opposite) Patrols seem to be mostly for gathering information about neighbors and trying to unsettle them. A tall tree offers a rare opportunity to look over other territory.

2. Sometimes, if chimpanzees are feeding near the edge of their territory, a group of males might suddenly and silently set off on a patrol into their neighbors' area.

overlap, and chance encounters with other chimpanzee groups are not unusual.

Chimpanzees will never attack a group if it includes two or more males, since there is no knowing how strong and dangerous they are. If they can tell from pant hoots that a much bigger group is near, the patrolling chimpanzees will try to slip away quietly. When they get back into familiar ground, the patrol dissolves, and the chimpanzees seem to release tension by bursting into vigorous displays and loud calls.

If the two groups seem to be equally matched, they display from a safe distance with a salvo of "waa barks" and pant hoots. They then listen to the response from the other group. Eventually they withdraw noisily to their core area. The patrol has served its purpose, which is to remind neighbors of their presence. There is no violence, and no one gets hurt. It is just a lot of posturing.

However, if the patrolling chimpanzees come upon a lone male or a couple of females, they attack brutally. If many such attacks end in death, the effects can, over time, be dramatic. The whole community can be wiped out. This is what happened at Gombe during what was dubbed the "four-year war." Males from the northern Kasakela community killed all seven of the adult males from the southern Kahama community, along with the matriarch, Madam Bee, and several other adult females. The Kasakela community then spread over the old Kahama range, taking in surviving adult and adolescent females and their young.

The Kasakela chimpanzees did not enjoy their new space for long. The old Kahama community

1

1. Chimpanzees keep track of who else is in the vicinity by calling and listening for a response.

2. In a hunt, the drivers get the colobus monkeys moving through the canopy, while the blockers close off possible escape routes. The chasers then move in for the catch, and the ambusher completes the encirclement.

had acted as a buffer between them and a powerful community farther south. Within a year, these new neighbors had forced the Kasakela chimpanzees back up north, out of the Kahama territory that they had won so bloodily. The Kasakela chimps wound up with less territory than they had in the first place.

Hunting

Chimpanzees hunt wild pigs, deer, and monkeys, but their favorite prey is colobus monkeys. Monkeys are much smaller than chimpanzees and they can bound along thin branches that will not take a chimpanzee's weight. In the thick forest cover of Taï, the canopy is nearly continuous, and there are

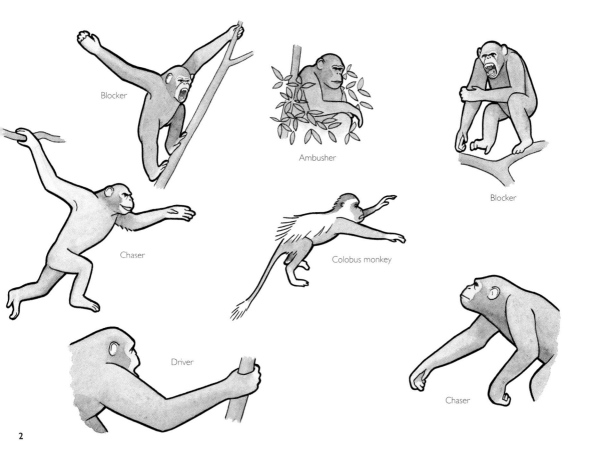

Blocker

Ambusher

Blocker

Chaser

Colobus monkey

Driver

Chaser

2

hundreds of escape routes for the monkeys, so the chimpanzees must cooperate closely if they are to stand a chance of catching one.

In a typical hunt, chimpanzee males take on one of four different roles. First, there are the "drivers," who get the colobus monkeys moving through the canopy without actually chasing them. Younger, less experienced males usually take this role. Meanwhile, the "blockers" take up their positions, conspicuously blocking any potential escape routes. Then the "chasers" swing into action. These chimpanzees may be the ones to catch the monkey

when it is driven into a particular tree. The blockers keep up, changing their positions depending on how things develop. Finally, there is the "ambusher," the job that requires the most experience, the most skill, and the best judgement. This chimpanzee rushes ahead and waits in the fleeing monkey's path, forcing it to turn around and face the killers.

Hunting occurs in all chimpanzee populations, but the rates vary enormously, as does the quantity of meat that is consumed. At Taï, chimpanzees hunt regularly, and kill an average of 125 colobus in

1

2

1. Fertile females join hunting parties and may take part in the kill. Gombe chimpanzee Gigi grins in excitement during a colobus hunt.

2. It takes years to learn to hunt. A male chimpanzee's apprenticeship starts at the age of 10, but he will not be a skilled hunter until he is 20.

 COLOBUS CONTROL

The group size and behavior of any animal is molded by the environment, how much food, water, and shelter there is. However, another species can also count as an environmental factor, and for red colobus monkeys, that species is the chimpanzee. Chimpanzees hunt tree-living red colobus monkeys. Usually, the prey is an infant snatched from its mother, or a juvenile too slow to escape. When attacked, colobus males cluster together to try to shield the females and young. They may leap onto the chimpanzees, bite, and chase them. Sometimes, if there are only a couple of chimpanzees, the colobus manage to fight them off but chimpanzees still kill large numbers of colobus. At Gombe, they are responsible for up to 35 percent of monkey deaths a year. Two thirds of these are infants and juveniles, therefore chimpanzees have a huge effect on the age structure of the colobus groups. They also affect the monkeys' social life. The more hunting there is by chimpanzees, the smaller the colobus groups are.

1. The hunters tear off chunks of colobus meat and crack open large bones to get the marrow.

2. This group, like Bonobo communities, are much larger than common chimpanzees', anywhere from 40 to 120 individuals.

1

If they find a fresh carcass, chimpanzees will not scavenge the meat. They make anxious, puzzled sounds, touching the corpse, then sniffing their fingers, like they do with a dead chimpanzee.

250 hunts per year. Chimpanzees at Gombe kill only about 66 colobus per year. In Budongo, Uganda, hunting has been seen only twice. In Bossou, Guinea, chimpanzees have been seen to hunt only five times in eight years. Even though meat has high nutritional value, it does not seem crucial to the chimpanzee's survival.

The exact way in which chimpanzees hunt varies between populations, too. Chimpanzees at Gombe are successful when hunting alone. Lone hunters there catch red colobus five times more often than lone Taï hunters.

MANIPULATING OTHERS

Since meat has exchange value as well as nutritional value, chimpanzees have the rudiments of a trade economy. Being able to buy favors this way, along with other forms of social manipulation, requires a developed sense of social awareness.

The feast at the end of a successful hunt is a highly social event. Typically, the chimpanzee who has caught the prey shares some of it with others, stripping meat from the carcass and handing it out. Lower-ranking chimpanzees frequently beg for meat from their superiors. The meat is not handed out equally or at random. The status of some males is confirmed, while that of others is undermined, and special friends get more, while those out of favor get less. Sometimes, the rigid dominance hierarchy is disrupted as the alpha male begs from subordinates. If fertile females are present, they may briefly become higher ranked than some males. ▷▷

2

Therefore, sharing food seems to be a way to repay or build debt and to curry favor. A powerful alpha male, Stogi, at Mahale, Tanzania, often caught monkeys and shared the meat with other chimpanzees, but he calculated the returns carefully. He gave meat only to older and middle-ranking males, never to young or senior males. What he appeared to be doing was servicing those relationships that were the most useful, with chimpanzees who would, in return, form coalitions against his rivals. He paid his supporters in meat.

Food-sharing may also sometimes be used to entice females. The chances of a hunting opportunity being taken at Gombe soars from 55 percent to near certainty if five or more fertile females are present. If the hunters catch something, the females are almost sure to get some meat, and they are more likely to mate with males who are generous. This is especially the case at Taî, where females enjoy a high status when it comes to meat-sharing.

Previous page: Whether a chimpanzee is successful at begging for meat from another at the end of a hunt depends on the relationship, their relative age and rank, and how much meat there is to go around.

1. At Gombe, Passion and her family feast on an infant chimpanzee.

2. Chimpanzees keep careful social accounts. The alpha's ally will switch allegiance if he does not get special privileges.

Social intelligence

To cope with the ever changing social tangle that the "fission-fusion" lifestyle promotes, chimpanzees must be able to make split-second decisions about how to behave. For a start, they must recognize other individuals and anticipate what might happen next, as a disturbing story from Gombe illustrates. In a rare cannabalistic attack, high-ranking female Passion killed and ate Gilka's first baby. When, a year later, Passion approached Gilka and her second baby, Gilka screamed. She was right to be terrified, as Passion killed and ate that baby, too.

⭐ It seems that chimpanzees cannot keep a straight face. They sometimes try to hide their play face when they want to keep their playful intentions from another animal.

2

Chimpanzees must also appreciate where they stand with other individuals, so that they can work out how to behave. And they must know what is going on between others: who are allies, who are rivals, and who are related, as these third-party relationships might have consequences for them, too. Social awareness in chimps is particularly important because so much of their life revolves around complex interactions between three or more individuals. Each must know not only how it relates to the others, but how they all relate to one another. For example, at Gombe, subordinate chimpanzees

knew to treat Faben with great respect, at least when his alpha brother was around.

This level of understanding means that chimpanzees can manipulate each other. Pooch, a young female at Gombe, reached for one of the bananas that high-ranking female Circe was eating, and Circe threatened her. Pooch left, screaming, to return a few moments later with the old male Huxley, with whom she had a special friendship. With Huxley behind her, Pooch threatened Circe, who moved away. Pooch had used her relationship with Huxley as a social tool. Pooch recognized that

Circe was higher-ranking than her but lower-ranking than Huxley, and she knew Huxley would back her up. She therefore took advantage of her relationship with Huxley and the difference in dominance between him and Circe to achieve her original goal.

Deception

From this kind of behavior, it seems a short step to deception. A young chimp might let out a fear-scream, not because it is scared of anything, but because it wants to attract its mother's attention and ride on her back. When Figan was a young male, he learned to control his reaction to food. If big males heard his excitement when researchers smuggled bananas to him, they would certainly relieve him of them. Figan would suppress his loud food-grunts so that they were no more than soft sounds at the back of his throat.

An individual may feign lack of interest in order to mislead another. Meat-loving Flo sat near her son Figan for nearly a quarter of an hour apparently ignoring him as he ate a colobus carcass. She edged closer, looking away all the time and grooming herself. When she was within arm's reach, she made a lunge for the meat, but Figan was prepared and leapt away. Figan was also skilled at leading other chimpanzees away from bananas when he had not been able to get to any. He would stride off in a way

 GROOMING

In grooming, one chimpanzee parts another one's hair to expose the skin. Then, peering in with concentration, picks out and eats bits of dirt, scabs, ticks, and other foreign bodies, often with exaggerated tooth-clacking or lip-smacking noises. Particularly among unrelated chimpanzees, it is loaded with significance. Adult males tend to groom higher-ranking males more than they get groomed in return. Friends groom each other a lot. If the atmosphere between them becomes tense, two males will groom each other in an attempt to diffuse things. Adult females groom just about everyone in their family. Grooming can mean caring, respect, submission, courtship, and much more. Who grooms whom, for how long, and when, matters deeply. This simple action is the single most powerful social tool.

1. Social manipulation is a sophisticated skill. A begging chimpanzee must be careful not to push its luck too far.

that suggested that he knew of a good food source. When they had followed him, Figan would lose them and double back to eat the bananas.

All these examples suggest intentional deception, but it may be that the "liar" does not actually intend to deceive its victim. An infant who screams in "fear" when it wants to be carried may once have been genuinely frightened by something and was carried as a result. The infant then only has to associate fear-screams with being carried and it produces them whenever it feels tired. Though the mother is "deceived" into carrying, that is, she picks the infant up because she thinks it is frightened, this is only functional, not intentional, deception. The infant is not consciously attempting to deceive its mother; it is simply producing a behavior that, in the past, has led to its being carried.

But so often, chaimpanzee behavior seems to suggest a deliberate strategy to deceive. Younger males will often lead females out of sight of high-ranking males to mate with them. The females also learn to muffle their copulation squeals. It seems that both must have some idea of how the alpha male would react if he were to catch them.

Manipulating other chimpanzees, whether it is by straightforward communication or through the tactics of food sharing, grooming or deception, is much of what being a wild chimpanzee is all about. They are, above all, highly social animals. Amazing as they are as individuals, it is only when they are in their natural context with other chimpanzees in the wild that their true potential unfolds. It is a privilege that only 200,000 wild chimpanzees now enjoy. In terms of conservation, they are precious indeed.

FURTHER INFORMATION

BOOKS

Christophe Boesch and Hedwige Boesch-Acherman, *The Chimpanzees of the Tai Forest: Behavioral Ecology and Evolution* (Oxford University Press, 2000)

Paola Cavalieri & Peter Singer (eds), *The Great Ape Project* (Fourth Estate Ltd, 1993)

Jared Diamond, *The Rise and Fall of the Third Chimpanzee* (Vintage, 1992)

Jane Goodall, *In the Shadow of Man* (Collins, 1971)

Jane Goodall, *The Chimpanzees of Gombe: Patterns of Behavior* (The Belknap Press of Harvard University Press, 1986)

Jane Goodall, *Through a Window* (Weidenfeld & Nicolson, 1990)

Jane Goodall, *My Life with the Chimpanzees* (Pocket Books, 1988)

Jane Goodall (with Philip Berman) *Reason for Hope* (Thorsons, 1999)

P. Heltne & L. Marquardt, *Understanding Chimpanzees* (Harvard University Press, 1989)

T. Kano, *The Last Ape* (Stanford University Press, 1992)

Tess Lemmon, *Chimpanzees* (Whittet Books, 1994)

W. C. McGrew, *Chimpanzee*

Material Culture: Implications for Human Evolution (Cambridge University Press, 1992)

Michael Nichols and Jane Goodall, *Brutal Kinship* (Aperture Foundation)

Dale Peterson and Jane Goodall, *Visions of Caliban – on Chimpanzees and People* (The University of Georgia Press, revised edition, 2000)

Frans de Waal, *Chimpanzee Politics* (The Johns Hopkins University Press, revised edition 1998)

R. W. Wrangham, W. C. McGrew, Frans B. de Waal & Paul G. Heltne (eds), *Chimpanzee Cultures* (Harvard University Press, 1994)

MAGAZINE

BBC Wildlife Magazine
A monthly look at wildlife and conservation world wide.

WEBSITES

The Jane Goodall Institute-UK
15 Clarendon Park
Lymington Hants SO41 8AX
Tel: 01590 671188 Fax: 670887
e-mail: info@janegoodall.org.uk
www.janegoodall.org

The International Primate Protection League-UK
116 Judd Street
London WC1H 9NS
020 7833 0661
enquiries@ippl-uk.org
www.ippl-uk.org

International Primatological Society
http://indri.primate.wisc.edu/pin/ips.html

INDEX

Italic type denotes illustrations